Christmastime in New York City

. . . .

Christmastime in New York City

ROXIE MUNRO

DODD, MEAD & COMPANY · NEW YORK

Thanks to Rosanne Lauer, my editor,
and Bo Zaunders, my husband.

Copyright © 1987 by Roxie Munro.
All rights reserved. No part of this book may be reproduced in any
form without permission in writing from the publisher.
Printed in The United States of America by Horowitz / Rae

1 2 3 4 5 6 7 8 9 10

Library of Congress Cataloging-in-Publication Data
Munro, Roxie.   Christmastime in New York City.
Summary: Presents panoramic drawings of various sights
in New York City during the Christmas season including
the Thanksgiving Day Parade, decorated shop windows,
and the New Year's Eve celebration in Times Square.
1. Christmas – New York (N.Y.) – Pictorial works.
2. Christmas decorations – New York (N.Y.) – Pictorial
works.   3. New York (N.Y.) – Social life and customs –
Pictorial works.   [1. Christmas – New York (N.Y.) –
Pictorial works.   2. Christmas decorations – New York
(N.Y.) – Pictorial works.   3. New York (N.Y.) – Social
life and customs – Pictorial works]   I. Title.
GT4986.N7M86   1987   394.2'68282'097471   86-32914
ISBN 0-396-08909-7

For Andrew, Aaron, Robbie, Johan, Joacim, and Jennica

. . . .

Macy's Thanksgiving Day Parade

The Metropolitan Museum of Art

Rockefeller Plaza

South Street Seaport

Radio City Music Hall®

Lord & Taylor Windows

Lord & Taylor Windows

Park Avenue

The New York Public Library

FAO Schwarz

Manhattan Skyline

Saint Thomas Church

Times Square

MACY'S THANKSGIVING DAY PARADE was originated by Macy's employees in 1924. Many employees were first-generation immigrants, eager to celebrate their new American heritage in a manner similar to festivals in their native lands. From its beginnings with live animals borrowed from the Central Park Zoo, floats, and bands, it has been a huge success. The popular balloons were added in 1927, with additions and changes each year. The Parade was suspended only during the war years of 1942 to 1944. It runs from 77th Street and Central Park West down Broadway to 34th Street and Seventh Avenue.

THE METROPOLITAN MUSEUM OF ART is located at 82nd Street and Fifth Avenue. The building first opened in 1880. Since 1965, from December 5 through January 4 each year, the Angel Tree has been erected in the Medieval Court Hall. The tree, a thirty-foot blue spruce, is decorated with angels and cherubs, and at its base are almost two hundred Nativity figurines. The figurines were collected by Loretta Hines Howard, beginning in the 1920s. In 1965, the first tree was created by her, a tradition that is carried on by her daughter, Linn Howard Selby. The Museum is open Tuesday – 9:30 A.M.-8:45 P.M. (except holidays), Wednesday through Sunday – 9:30 A.M.-5:15 P.M. It is closed on Monday.

ROCKEFELLER CENTER encompasses an area from approximately 48th Street to 51st Street between Fifth Avenue and Avenue of the Americas. The tradition of a tree at the Plaza began in the middle of the Great Depression. In 1931, with the foundations being laid for several of the Center's first buildings, a group of construction workers set up a Christmas tree. This was the start of a yearly celebration that begins with the selection of a special tree, which is decorated with 20,000 lights. The tree is lit in early December each year. Since 1981, the Channel Gardens leading to the tree have contained twelve herald angels, which are eight-feet tall wire sculptures.

SOUTH STREET SEAPORT, at Fulton and Water streets, is a restored area in the cultural heart of New York City. The Seaport was once called the "Street of Ships." The South Street Seaport Museum (207 Front Street) sponsors programs on its piers, aboard its historic ships, on the cobblestone streets, and in its gallery. During the Christmas season special events are planned, such as Lamplight Tours, Wagonette Rides, a strolling Santa Claus, and a "Chorus Tree," a 65-member choir dressed in red and green.

RADIO CITY MUSIC HALL® is located at 1260 Avenue of the Americas. It opened its doors on December 27, 1932, with its first Christmas show being produced the following year. From 1933 until 1979, each Christmas show combined a movie with a live stage show. In 1979, Radio City Music Hall® began offering a ninety-minute, all-live stage presentation for Christmas. Since that time, "The Parade of the Wooden Soldiers" featuring the Rockettes®, its precision dance team of thirty-six, has been a part of the show.

LORD & TAYLOR, a department store between 38th and 39th streets on Fifth Avenue, has decorated its windows with animated scenes of New York City for the past thirty years. The ones pictured in this book are from the 1986 Christmas season, featuring historically accurate period recreations with over ninety costumed figures. The windows include scenes of The Main Reading Room Foyer of the New York Public Library in 1911; a Christmas reception at the Frick Collection, Fragonard Room, in 1936; The Metropolitan Museum of Art, showing its original Victorian Gothic Building in 1874; and The Museum of the City of New York, 1932, with its collection of antique toys and dolls. The windows are usually unveiled the week before Thanksgiving and remain on view until New Year's Day.

PARK AVENUE. Since 1944, a line of Christmas trees has been illuminated in the center island of Park Avenue. It extends from 53rd Street to 96th Street. The trees are lighted on December 7 and usually remain lighted until Twelfth Night, January 6. First begun by Mrs. Steven Clark, as a memorial to our country's war dead, the tradition is continued by an anonymous donor.

THE NEW YORK PUBLIC LIBRARY has its Central Research facility at Fifth Avenue between 41st and 42nd streets. At Christmastime, the two guardian lions of the library are wreathed for the holiday season. The lions were sculpted from pink Tennessee marble by Edward C. Potter in 1911. Originally called "Leo Astor" and "Leo Lenox" after the New York Public Library founders, John Jacob Astor and James Lenox, their nicknames have changed over the decades. They were named "Patience" (south side) and "Fortitude" (north side) by Mayor Fiorello LaGuardia during the Depression of the 1930s. To New Yorkers, they are simply known as the "Library Lions."

FAO SCHWARZ is a toy store located at 767 Fifth Avenue, in the General Motors Building. Founded in 1862, there are now twenty-one branches across the country with boutiques in the B. Altman's department stores.

NEW YORK CITY SKYLINE from Brooklyn Heights, showing the Brooklyn Bridge (foreground) and the Manhattan Bridge. Lighted for Christmas are the Empire State Building and The Metropolitan Life Building.

SAINT THOMAS CHURCH is an Episcopal church located on Fifth Avenue at 53rd Street. The parish was first organized in 1823 by a group of laymen. After the third church was destroyed by fire in 1905, the present Gothic structure was built, and it was dedicated in 1916. Every Christmas Eve at 4:00 P.M., the Nativity scene is recreated, with the children of the parish participating. This event has been going on since the church was founded.

TIMES SQUARE is located at 42nd Street between Broadway and Seventh Avenue. The descent of a lighted ball on a pole from the top of 1 Times Square at midnight on New Year's Eve has been virtually unchanged since it began in 1908. The idea for a ball came from a 1905 celebration which was climaxed by fireworks. Because of an accident, fireworks became illegal and a new safe and spectacular way to celebrate had to be found. The original designer of the ball was Jacob Starr. At one minute before the New Year, the lighted ball, which has become an apple with 180 red lights in recent years, begins its descent down the pole. At the stroke of midnight, the beginning of the New Year, the ball reaches the bottom of the pole and the date of the New Year lights up. The celebration was interrupted only during the years of 1943 and 1944. From 250,000 to 500,000 spectators crowd into the Times Square area for the party every year.